General J.O. Shelby
at Clarendon, Arkansas

The Capture and Destruction
of the U.S.S. *Queen City*

Don Roth

ISBN: 978-1-929919-77-2

Camp Pope Publishing
PO Box 2232
Iowa City, Iowa 52244
www.camppope.com

Cover art by Cecilia Putter

Contents

Illustrations

Foreword

It can be said that the American Civil War has drawn more interest and historical scholarship than any other event in our nation's past. The War as it was fought west of the Mississippi River has perhaps been the least covered of all the aspects of the conflict. *General J. O. Shelby at Clarendon, Arkansas: The Capture and Destruction of the USS* Queen City addresses the cauldron of lawlessness generated by deserters from both sides behind enemy lines, while highlighting the destruction of the USS *Queen City* by Gen. Joseph O. Shelby. This 1864 event on the lower White River, 50 miles from the Mississippi River, marks the only sinking of a Federal warship in Arkansas waters. Considered one of the best Confederate cavalrymen to operate in the Trans-Mississippi, Shelby led his "Iron Brigade" on one of the longest cavalry raids of the Civil War.

Author Don Roth is a U. S. Air Force veteran who became active in the Grand Prairie Historical Society upon his retirement 25 years ago. He has remained active in preservation efforts and is a contributor to the *Grand Prairie Historical Bulletin*, with highly-researched subjects on Civil War topics near Stuttgart, his Arkansas County hometown. Roth initiated the placement of a substantial historical marker commemorating Missouri Gen. Mosby M. Parsons, who encamped his command almost within present-day Stuttgart during September 1862, while transferring his men from the State Guard into the Confederacy. The author has established a marker honoring the leader of a redoubtable Texas recon group near St Charles, 35 miles below Clarendon. He is active in history preservation efforts at Helena, Arkansas.

In *General J. O. Shelby at Clarendon*, the author highlights his subject's talent in both the tactical and strategic aspect of cavalry operations. Roth endeavors to humanize as many of the players as possible with photographs some of which are published for the first time. I am not well-read

Don Roth

on Civil War history, but after reading *Shelby at Clarendon*, I hope you will enjoy the book as much as I did.

H. Glenn Mosenthin
Editor and Board Member, Grand Prairie Historical Society

Preface

At an early age in grade school, while studying the Arkansas history text, I noticed General Shelby was the only successful Southern officer in a state full of military failures during the Civil War.

I was already interested in the Civil War near home from the time I first heard the two words. Many were the small unit actions where Shelby triumphed. The awkward attempt of this first time author is to construct a book length treatment on one such exploit that occurred during 1864 on the lower White River in Arkansas. Analysis is made in the latter portion of the book to justify a point or conclusion.

I wish to thank the staffs of the National Archives in Washington, D. C. for their assistance. My gratitude also extends to the fine people at Wilson's Creek National Battlefield Museum, the Butler Center for Arkansas Studies, in Little Rock, and the U. S. Naval History and Heritage Command. The editorial skills of Mr. Ron Kelly and Mr. Glenn Mosenthin guided me toward the publication process. To them I am most appreciative but no less so to the librarians La Tiffany Henderson and Estelle Dudman, and finally Randy Puckett whose technical assistance helped to made this work possible.

Major General Frederick Steele. Following the blunderous Red River operations in southwest Arkansas that came to a head in the swollen swamps of the Saline River bottoms at Jenkins Ferry on April 30, 1864, General Steele began dealing with Confederate cavalry under J. O. Shelby in the White River valley. *Courtesy of the Library of Congress.*

Chapter One

When Union Major-General Frederick Steele entered the Little Rock fortifications as head of the Seventh Army Corp on May 3, 1864, this terminated his association with the Red River Campaign. The futile operation was a concentric advance reluctantly endorsed by Lieutenant-General Ulysses Simpson Grant, General-In-Chief of all Federal forces. Steele's role in the peculiar expedition was to form a juncture with Major-General Nathaniel Prentis Banks, who was ascending the Red River in Louisiana to seize cotton and the industrial city of Shreveport. On March 23, Gen. Steele's army of approximately 8500 troops advanced southwest from Little Rock to assist with the seizure of that city, which also served as the headquarters of the Trans-Mississippi Department commander, Lieutenant-General Edmund Kirby Smith.[1]

By April 15, Steele found himself surrounded in Camden by the army of Major-General Sterling Price, Commander of the District of Arkansas. On April 18, a courier got through to inform Steele that General Banks' column was blunted at Mansfield,

Lt.-General Edmund Kirby Smith, Confederate Trans-Mississippi Department Commander. *Courtesy of the Library of Congress.*

1. Ludwell H. Johnson, *The Red River Campaign: Politics and Cotton in the Civil War* (Baltimore: The Johns Hopkins University Press, 1958), 4–5, 8, 10, 44–47; U. S. Grant, *Personal Memoirs of U. S. Grant*, 2 vols. (New York: Charles L. Webster & Company, 1885), 2:139.

Major-General Sterling Price, Commander of the District of Arkansas. *Courtesy of the Library of Congress.*

Louisiana on April 9, and compelled to turn back. Facing serious logistical problems that made his position untenable, General Steele secretly evacuated his half-starving army from Camden on the night of April 26. The campaign cost him fearfully in men, artillery and transportation.[2]

As the dust settled, General Grant instructed Steele to engage the enemy only to protect the Arkansas River line. Steele's right flank began at Fort Smith on the Arkansas River near today's Oklahoma state line. It extended east to centrally located Little Rock, with small garrisons in between. Forty-five miles downstream from the capital was Union-occupied Pine Bluff. In 1864 the U. S. Navy maintained an infrequent presence on the lowest portion of this fickle river on which Steele could only seasonally rely.

General Sterling Price faded from the Red River Campaign after battling Steele's retreating army at a swollen Saline River crossing thirty-five miles from Little Rock on April 30. His superior, General Kirby Smith, ordered his infantry divisions south to co-operate in an effort to drive Banks from Louisiana, but arrived too late to be of any assistance. Smith then assigned a brigade of Price's Missouri cavalry division to Chicot County in extreme southeast Arkansas to harry and disrupt Mississippi River navigation.[3]

The remaining brigade commanded by the charismatic and newly promoted Brigadier-General Joseph Orville (Jo) Shelby, received a intensely challenging assignment; he was ordered to occupy the White River valley

2. Steele's total losses in the campaign amounted to 2750 casualties, nine field guns and over 650 wagons. William C. Davis in Patricia Faust (ed.) *Historical Times Illustrated Encyclopedia of the Civil War* (New York: Harper & Row, 1986), 107.
3. The rear assault launched against Steele's retreating army on the Saline River was known as the Battle of Jenkins Ferry.

behind General Steele's lines. The primary reason was to organize loose military personnel, conscripts and recalcitrant deserters into serviceable commands, besides exterminating robbers, jayhawkers and other predatory bands. He was also tasked to disrupt Steele's supply line by annoying White River navigation and wrecking the railroad linking Little Rock with DeValls Bluff, the big supply base situated on that stream. These measures could certainly compound General Steele's already painful logistical problems.[4]

Although reduced in number by the month-long campaign against the Federals, Shelby's men were full of fight. Artillery Captain Richard Armstrong Collins was especially satisfied, because his battery had gained two fine ten-pounder parrot rifles in an April 15 wagon train capture at Marks' Mill, which occurred thirty-five miles southwest of Pine Bluff.[5]

***

SHELBY WAS A PRE-WAR BUSINESSMAN in Waverly, Missouri who shared a partnership with a kinsman in the hemp industry. He began the War in 1861 by declining a Federal commission in favor of leading a cavalry company in the Missouri State Guard, an organization commanded by General Price, when he launched his own career fighting to hold Missouri for the Confederacy. This wasn't accomplished, because the Confederate army he was serving was ordered to cross the Mississippi River to assist in an effort that culminated in the battle of Shiloh. All cavalry including Captain Shelby's company were dismounted and sweltered in northern Mississippi.

Five months later on September 22, 1862, Shelby, with the rank of Colonel, was given command of three cavalry regiments primarily from as many Missouri counties, one he personally recruited near his home in Lafayette County. This Lexington, Kentucky native had no formal military

---

4. U. S. War Department , *The War of the Rebellion: A Compilation of the Official Records of the Union and Confederate Armies (128 vols. Washington D. C, 1880–1901),* Series I, Vol. 34, Part 1:191–92 (hereafter cited as *ORA*); Unless otherwise indicated, all references are to Series I, Volume 34, Part 1. Jayhawkers were Union guerilas who were notorious for anti-Confederate sentiment.
5. The Battle of Marks' Mill was the turning point of the expedition.

training, but the efficiency of his command matured rapidly under his energetic leadership.[6]

A recent biographer described the following tactical implementation employed by Colonel Shelby against Kansas abolitionist General James G. Blunt at Cane Hill in northwest Arkansas:

> Known since ancient times but seldom employed successfully because it required exquisite timing and implementation, the fighting retreat became Shelby's trademark. Shelby had designed the tactic and worked out its execution earlier, in particular the communications techniques between company commanders and himself. He first used it to stun the capable Union general James Blunt in November 1862. Blunt's two brigades of some five thousand men outnumbered Shelby by five to two as they pursued him into the Boston Mountains of north-west Arkansas. Taking advantage of the thickly wooded terrain, Shelby deployed his thirty companies every two hundred yards. The first company fired on the Federal advance unit, then broke off and quickly retreated to the end of the defensive line. The next company did the same, then the third, and so on down the line, preventing the enemy's main body from getting close enough to do real harm. The Federals could lay claim to terrain that Shelby's men gave up in this manner, but at considerable cost in terms of soldiers killed and wounded—and above all, in time lost.[7]

Here in the rugged terrain of Washington County, Arkansas, Shelby's Missouri Cavalry Brigade began to define itself. Additionally this skillful rear guard operation bought precious time that allowed the army's flour laden commissary train to safely reach Van Buren on the Arkansas River. During half the war's entirety, Shelby's tactical expertise appeared to stave off destruction that his superiors brought upon themselves through their inability to lead cavalry with competence.

---

6. After the War, the organization, inclusive with a scouting battalion and a four-gun battery, became known as "Shelby's Iron Brigade." Deryl Sellmeyer, *Jo Shelby's Iron Brigade* (Gretna LA: Pelican Publishing, 2007), 302.

7. Anthony Arthur, *General Jo Shelby's March* (New York: Random House, 2010), 31.

General J. O. Shelby at Clarendon, Arkansas

General Shelby's grasp of the strategic role of the mounted arm was effectively demonstrated during September and October of 1863, when he staged a successful raid from Arkadelphia, Arkansas to the Missouri River, where he watered his horses in a likely gesture of triumph. The swift 1,500-mile rampage was more extensive than any mounted raid in the war and averaged an inconceivable thirty-six miles a day. The route of march was regulated by the selection of small targets while avoiding pitched battles. In this way with celerity and surprise, Shelby kept his troops well supplied with the finest weapons, fresh horses and warm uniforms. However, this unlikely but well-documented event of thirty-six miles a day wasn't enough

Captain John Jarrette. Southern guerrillas like Jarrette contributed to the stealth of the 1863 Missouri raid by smashing enemy courier escorts sent off when telegraph service was disrupted. *Courtesy of Missouri Valley Special Collections, Kansas City Public Library.*

to allow him the political goal of hoisting the Confederate flag atop the Capitol dome in heavily defended Jefferson City. Nor was his 1,200-man force large enough to effect any strategic advantage in the Trans-Mississippi Department, but the raid demonstrated what he could achieve when left to his own devices. Later there were claims the raiding expedition prevented the Federals from transferring large numbers of troops to reinforce Major-General William Rosecrans at Chattanooga, Tennessee. Jo Shelby didn't excel quietly—he was a braggart and a showoff. Nonetheless he was rewarded with a general's star not long after returning to Arkansas.[8]

---

8. Roy Bird, "Jo Shelby and His Shadow," *America's Civil War* 8 (March 1995): 29.

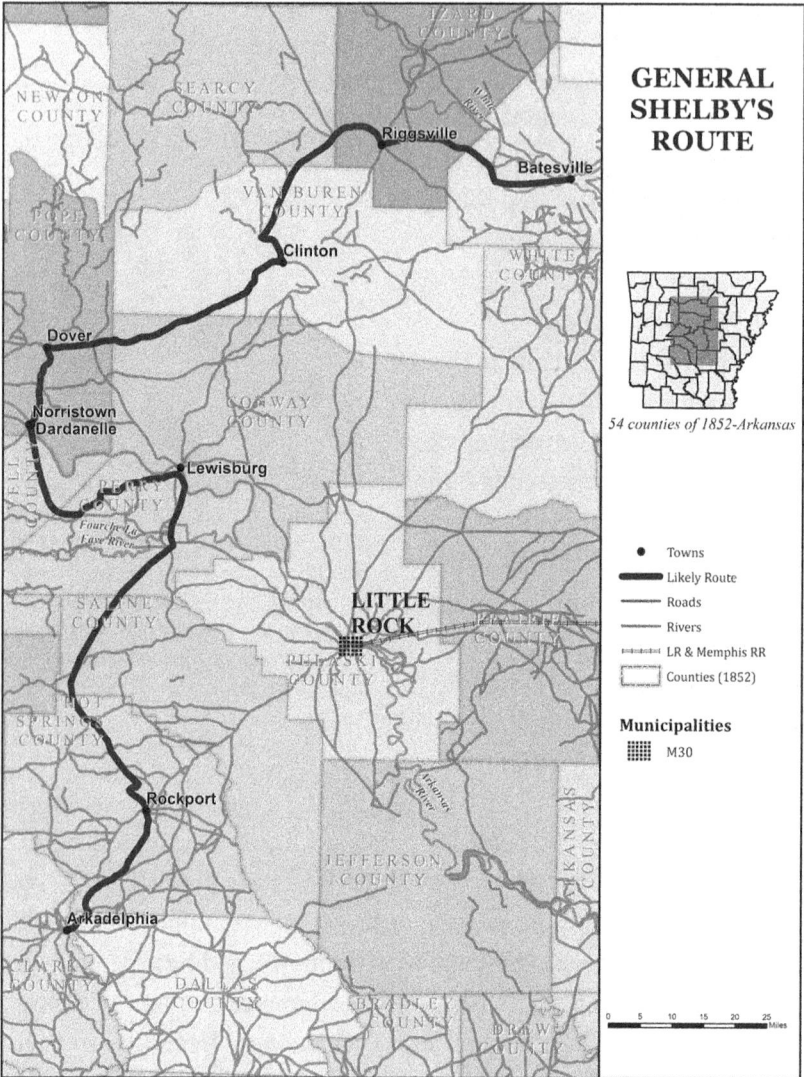

This is the brutal route pursued by General J.O. Shelby to pierce General Steele's Arkansas River line. His march began on May 9, 1864 and he pierced the line on May 17 and 18. The march terminated twelve miles from Batesville on May 26, 1864. *Map by Randy Puckett.*

Chapter Two

Assuming the increased responsibility that came with promotion, he rode north from Camp Bullock near Arkadelphia on May 9. Lieutenant-Colonel Benjamin C. Elliot's First Missouri Battalion was tasked with scouting ahead. This former Virginian and VMI graduate moved to California for a short stay, then bought a farm in Bates County, Missouri. He rose to the rank of Colonel in the State Guard, but transferred into the Confederacy on joining Shelby's brigade in September, 1862 and led a scouting company with the rank of Captain. [9]

The rest of the brigade consisted as follows: the Fifth Missouri Cavalry Regiment was commanded by Colonel Benjamin Franklin Gordon. This 38-year-old Mexican War veteran had once operated a drugstore down the street from the firm of Shelby & Gratz in Waverly, Missouri, a city that overlooked the river by that name. He was also an original member of Captain Shelby's mounted company while in the State Guard.[10] The Eleventh Missouri Cavalry Regiment in 1864 was commanded by Colonel Moses W. Smith. A farmer by occupation, this twenty-six-year-old Maine native was promoted through the ranks from Private. He was killed

Benjamin Elliot, VMI Cadet, ca. 1851. *Courtesy of Virginia Military Institute Archives.*

9. Bruce S. Allardice, *Confederate Colonels: A Biographical Register* (Columbia, MO and London: University of Missouri Press, 2008), 139.
10. Ibid., 169

15

COL. DAVID SHANKS.

Colonel David Shanks. *Confederate Veteran Magazine.*

in action near Newtonia, Missouri on October 28, 1864.[11]

The Twelfth Missouri Cavalry Regiment was commanded by Colonel David Shanks, a combat-driven officer who often led from the front and had the scars of fourteen wounds to show for it. He went on to command the brigade when Shelby took charge of a division during Price's 1864 Raid. Colonel Shanks was severely wounded and captured near Jefferson City on October 6, 1864.[12] And there was Collins' Battery of four guns. Of 23 year old Captain Richard Armstrong Collins, not much is known except he was a Kentuckian by birth and completed higher education in Ohio. A number of substandard ordinance wagons stood ready, of which one-third never reached the Arkansas River. In all, the column amounted to about 1,200 troops.[13]

General Shelby's Brigade experienced little trouble piercing the Arkansas River line at Dardanelle on May 17 and 18. They also met little resistance at a small garrison commanded by Colonel Abraham H. Ryan of the Third Arkansas Cavalry (US) near Lewisburg, now Morrilton. While moving rapidly northeast through mountainous Pope and Van Buren Counties, scouting detachments uncovered and executed bushwhackers and other predatory bands. The column hastened through Richwoods, Riggsville (Mountain View), and Buckhorn (now St. James), over the worst of roads. Burned-out dwellings and outright lawlessness

11. Ibid., 347.
12. Ibid., 340; Saber wounds weren't uncommon in mounted service. Shanks service record also reveals three gunshot wounds.
13. *ORA*, 839, 925.

gave evidence of a brutal and wasted countryside that was nothing short of appalling. Scouting parties continuously collided with bands of robbers and deserters, who were summarily dealt with. To make matters worse, one of the Parrott guns twice broke an axle, and had to be hauled in a wagon. The nightmare march of ninety circuitous miles finally ended after crossing the White River twelve miles above Batesville on May 26, where a Federal garrison had departed for DeValls Bluff a few days before.[14] The White River Valley was indeed a viper's nest of lawlessness and apathy—the sort of hell hole that accelerated a new meaning to the word nightmare.

The Federal high command was beset with rumors of the enemy's destination, and at one time settled upon the ridiculous belief that the enemy had turned back to re-cross the Arkansas. The Confederate incursion was later interpreted as an effort to attack the railroad. By May 25, it was discovered by Federal authorities that General Shelby had ridden north and around pursuing forces in the direction of Batesville.[15]

A week later an unsettled Shelby fired off a report to General Price at District HQ with portions presented herewith:

> The country is and has been pitiable in the extreme; Confederate soldiers in nothing save the name, robbers and Jayhawkers have vied with the Federals in plundering, devouring, and wasting the subsistence of loyal Southerners, and new cruelties have been devised to torture from unwilling lips the secret of some treasure. The entire valley is swept bare of forage and substance, and there are hundreds of families that must suffer for bread. I am forced for the first time in the history of war to graze my horses and feed my men on meat alone. In three weeks the wheat crop will be ready for use; but until that time we will be compelled to live on meat alone. The condition of so called Confederate forces here was horrible in the extreme—no organi-

---

14. *ORA*, 1050.
15. Ibid., 839, 925; David E. Casto, *Arkansas Late in the Civil War: The 8th Missouri Volunteer Cavalry, April, 1864–July, 1865* (Charleston, SC: The History Press, 2013), 41–43.

zation, no concentration, no discipline, no law, no leader, no anything. The seeds of cotton speculation, horse stealing, illicit and pernicious trading with the Federals was carried on with a high hand, thereby debauching the officers and demoralizing the men. They are scattered from Yellville to Helena, from the Missouri line to the Arkansas River, five or six to a house, sweltering in the fumes of Memphis whisky, and riding rough-shod over defenseless families on stolen horses, while predatory bands of Federals unmolested and unfought, roamed about like devouring wolves and swept whole neighbor-hoods at a breath. Many good Southern families fled to the various posts for protection and they were not to blame. Thus was the country devoured; and now when a regular Confederate force comes up to their help they find an enemy worse than armed men—starvation. [16]

While enroute to Batesville, recruiting authority was given to Captains and others of higher rank. After establishing headquarters on the north bank of the White, between Batesville and Jacksonport, Shelby expanded further on the business of recruiting and organization. With the firmness of an indomitable will, he ordered those who claimed authority to report to him where he then exhorted them to unite, and declared he was rigidly enforcing the conscription law and wanted every man between the ages of 17 and 50 for military duty. The general further admonished:

16. *ORA*; 925; Alan Thompson, "'Frank and Outspoken in my Disposition': The Wartime Letters of General Dandridge McRae," *Arkansas Historical Quarterly* 72 (Winter 2013): 363. When the Confederate presence left northeast Arkansas to protect Little Rock, bandits trickled in from the mountain counties. The problem expanded further when numbers of Port Hudson parolees arrived after that place capitulated in July 1863. When General Price evacuated Little Rock without a pitched battle on September 10, 1863, many troops from northeast Arkansas deserted and returned to their homes, and some descended into criminality thus described. Also Southern guerillas from Missouri withdrew into northern Arkansas to seek subsistence. As early as October 1, over one hundred Arkansas officers from Price's army from general on down were sent to the region to gather conscripts and deserters for removal back to the main army. All attempts were unsuccessful and only General Shelby's brigade, acting as a police force, proved effective at obtaining tangible results. Before summer's end, 8,000 troops were organized for hard service in Price's Missouri invasion.

"Tories and jayhawkers will be hanged and the people protected," before sending them off to beef up their ranks and joining Colonel McCray or wherever the Brigadier-General commanding directed.

In the weeks ahead, couriers were radiating throughout the country-side bearing stern edicts— if you were a deserter you had better rejoin either army. If you choose criminal behavior, expect to be shot on sight when caught in the act. Jacksonport was made the collection point and headquarters of Arkansas Colonel Thomas Hamilton McCray, who was tasked to organize the many unassigned companies and rag-tag parts of companies into battalions and regiments. He would later assemble a military board to try all accused offenders. By June 15, he was instructed by the iron-willed Shelby to use his own judgment in granting furloughs. The wheat crop was ready for harvest and the corn needed cultivating, and the general readily acknowledged the necessity of many soldiers to provide for their families. While this was going on, a steady southward movement commenced down the east side of White River by the Missouri cavalry brigade to provide subsistence for the horses while the grass lasted. After encamping for a short time below Augusta on a plantation within the Bell community, he revealed for the first time the main objective for the southward advance. He informed certain recruiting officers of a planned movement against the enemy requiring their immediate co-operation. A staff officer was sent from Shelby's headquarters to instruct each one concerning his own role in the operation.[17]

On June 19, despite heavy rains, Shelby pushed farther south while keeping his scouts busy toward Searcy and DeValls Bluff west of the White. This was necessary to protect his rear if Steele was bold enough to send a strike force to Jacksonport where Colonel McCray was trying to piece together a brigade from not yet viable units, while providing the men commissary and other quartermaster support. General Shelby was also concerned with the vulnerability of what remained of his ordnance and commissary wagons that survived the distressing march from Arkadelphia. Enemy scouting patrols, with few exceptions, had been

17. *ORA;* 928, 929; Vol. 34, Pt. 4:678, 680.

generally accurate in reporting his approximate locations and movements. However on June 18, Colonel Washington Franklin Geiger of the
Eighth Missouri Cavalry (US) reported from six miles below Clarendon
that Shelby was at Cotton Plant. But the Confederates on that date were
two days of reaching that village. Three days later, however, a battalion
commander from the Ninth Iowa Cavalry at Austin (Cabot), reported
Shelby with 1,500 men and artillery crossing the east running Little Red
River in detachments and were gathering at Hickory Plains, situated 14
miles equidistant of Austin and the White River community of Des Arc.
Now the role of the recruiting officers during Shelby's march became
evident. The rag-tag units and Southern guerrilla bands headed by recruiting officers were drawing attention to the Little Red, thus enabling
Shelby's column to steal a march down the east side of White River.[18]
While other cavalry detachments were looking out for enemy threats
from the direction of Missouri, Confederate Colonel Archibald Stephen-
son Dobbins of the First Arkansas Cavalry, who had long been operating in eastern Arkansas, was guarding the left flank from the direction
of Helena. Dobbins had also detailed junior officers to recruit, which often meant hunting down draft-dodgers hiding in the swamps, but on June 19, Dobbins was requested to call in his troops and rendezvous at Clarendon, the seat of Monroe County.[19]

A snapshot from the past would show Jo Shelby and his company trekking from eastern Mississippi and across Arkansas, on an awesome one thousand mile mission to recruit a cavalry regiment in the vicinity of Waverly Missouri. Their time in the

Colonel Archibald S. Dobbins. *Courtesy of Alabama Department of Archives and History, Montgomery, AL.*

18. Casto, *Arkansas Late in the Civil War,* 46.
19. *ORA,* 934.

Missouri State Guard expired on June 10, 1862, and the War Department in Richmond gave authorization to fulfill that mission. Along the way, civilian Shelby and company were entertained at the plantation home of Mr. and Mrs. Joel Lightfoot, some distance southeast of Clarendon. Five years later a former State Guard veteran would recall of the event, "a viands-loaded table amid heliotropes and roses in their dainty Southern home." After dinner Mrs. Lightfoot presented them a silk, hand-stitched Confederate battle flag before hastening on their way to Missouri, while bypassing Clarendon.[20]

The city of Clarendon was established in 1857, just before the county seat was moved to that location. By 1860, Monroe County's population had grown to 5,700, of which 2,200 were slaves. Cotton flourished, and census records show much of the population were native to Mississippi and Tennessee. Colonel James Harris and his brother, Senator Isham Harris, of the latter state, settled at Clarendon in 1856 and laid out the town the following year. Prior to the removal of the county seat to Clarendon, the location was known as "Mouth of Cache." The troublesome stream with its flooded bottomlands joined the White River about a quarter-mile above the town, and was now a great hindrance, and worse than General Price's disagreeable Helena expedition a year previous.

Upon the approach of the Civil War, Union sentiment mostly prevailed among the population county-wide. But when President Lincoln issued a call for volunteers, its citizens united with the Southern Confederacy. The first company of soldiers organized in Monroe County was commanded by Captain James Harris, followed by the organization of five additional infantry companies in 1861.[21] At this time in June, 1864, the survivors were a part of the Army of Tennessee, resisting Major-General William Tecumseh Sherman's juggernaut at Kennesaw Mountain, Georgia. In 1862, a few of Clarendon's sons had arrived to convalesce

---

20. John Newman Edwards, *Shelby and His Men or the War in the West* (Cincinnati, Miami Printing and Publishing Co., 1867), 266.
21. *Biographical and Historical Memoirs of Eastern Arkansas* (Chicago, Nashville, and St. Louis: Goodspeed Publishing Company, 1890), 512.

following the gruesome battle of Shiloh. Others returned to serve closer to home. Captain William Montgomery Mayo returned to raise a partisan company under the guidance of the April, 1862 Partisan Ranger Act, which gave authority to organize companies for irregular warfare. During the summer of 1864, he was employed by General Shelby as a guide and courier escort. Major John Benjamin Cocke of Clarendon commanded the advance of Brigadier General James Fleming Fagan's assault against a hilltop position (Battery "D") during the stormy July 4 Battle of Helena. He would later lose his life on the rain-swept killing field at Jenkins Ferry.

Incessant rains transformed the whole countryside into a vast lake, and the roads were in a condition worse than the June-July, 1863 mud march to Helena. That difficult expedition had been so severe, that General Price's infantry division struggled ten days to move sixty-five miles from Augusta to the river bastion. By sheer exertion, the four artillery pieces were crossed on some type of ferriage over the rolling Cache River on the night of June 20. The following day, after fording the Cache River bottom land, the brigade crossed the Bayou DeView Bridge before turning south toward Clarendon for a date with destiny.

This crossing bore similarities to the flooded Cache River bottoms. From *Battles and Leaders of the Civil War*, 4:213.

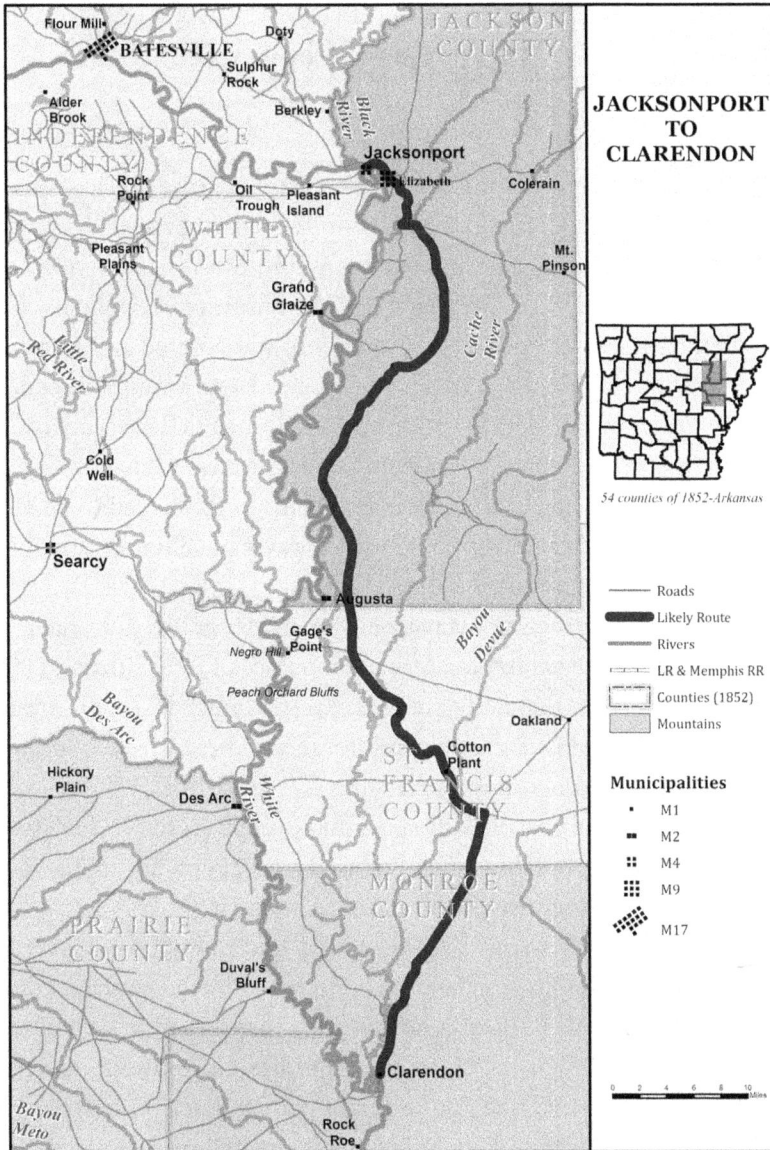

Map of General J.O. Shelby's route from Jacksonport to Clarendon. His march started on June 15 and concluded on June 24. His expedition was intended to interfere with navigation and transportation of military stores and troops on the White River. *Map by Randy Puckett.*

Chapter Three

On June 19, Lieutenant-Commander Seth Ledyard Phelps, of the Sixth District Mississippi Squadron, which embraced the White River fleet, gave verbal instructions to Acting Master's Mate Michael Hickey of the *USS Queen City* that firing at transports (steamboats) had been reported near the vicinity of Clarendon, and ordered him to patrol that area and keep a bright lookout at all times. Here, it might be added, the U. S. Navy was as adept at gathering intelligence as their army counterparts. The smaller tinclad gunboats had easy access to shallow inland streams that, in remote places, were far removed from roads, allowing deserters, Union sympathizers and escaped slaves to volunteer useful information without unwanted notice.

Hickey didn't confine all his patrolling activities entirely on water. At times his crew indulged in plundering the homes of local citizens. Once he confiscated from the pantry of Mrs. Sarah Kindel Sebastian several jars of molasses. Tiring of her demands for return, he invited her in company with other neighborhood women to search the boat. While escorting them around the vessel, a lady spied the coveted jars in a locked room through a knothole, but the Captain refused recovery of the pilfered food item and abruptly dismissed them from his gunboat.[22]

The *USS Queen City* was a side-wheeled tinclad gunboat converted from a Cincinnati Ohio ferryboat and purchased by the government in 1863 for $16,000. Also called light draughts, they were used extensively in western waterways including lakes and bayous to counter guerilla activity. The *Queen City* was clad in armor plating of 0.25-1.25 inches in thickness on the lower deck and portions of the hull, and displaced 212 tons of water, while maintaining a draft of approximately three to three and one-half feet. A lone 12-pounder was situated on the top deck, and

---

22. Author's interview with Mrs. Jo Claire English, July, 1974, in Clarendon, Arkansas.

U.S.S. Queen City. Courtesy of the U.S. Navy History and Heritage Command.

the gunboat mounted two 24-pounders and two 32-pounder naval guns broadside. Two 30-pounders occupied the bow, while two 24-pounders were positioned astern.[23] After brief service on the Tennessee and Cumberland Rivers, the gunboat participated in a portion of the Vicksburg Campaign before being assigned to the White River Fleet under the immediate supervision of Captain Hickey. Hickey was no stickler for regulations, but he possessed a strong realization of the vulnerability of his light draught. Every evening he insured his guns were primed for action, the decks well lighted, steam pressure maintained and guards posted. Also a slip was made on the anchor chain to allow instant withdrawal, in case an assailant proved too strong.[24]

---

23. J. Barto Arnold III, Texas Antiquities Committee Publication No. 6, *Beneath the Waters of Time: Proceedings of the Ninth Conference on Underwater Archeology*. n. d; Testimony given by Acting Masters Mate Michael Hickey, August 8, 1864, Vol. 161, Cases 4349–4358, *Records of General Courts Martials and Courts of Inquiry of the Navy Department, 1799–1867, Records of the National Archives Microfilm Publication*, Microcopy 273, Roll 170, Frames 0775–76; All references are made to roll 170. For a time Acting Masters Mate was the highest enlisted rank in the Union Navy. When commanding a boat the title "Captain" was given as a courtesy.

24. Testimony given by Executive Officer Fred M. Hathaway, August 8, 1864, Frame 0790.

At 10 PM on the night of June 23, a rifle went off on the top deck. Hickey learned from the officer of the watch that a guard thought he saw some men on horseback. Leaving nothing to chance, the captain ordered a reconnaissance into the town. This was accomplished by 30 sailors in three separate parties. They returned 80 minutes later, having found nothing unusual. What they didn't know however, was they had nearly collided with Col. Ben Elliot's scouts, who had been watching them intensely from the shadows.[25]

Earlier that evening Shelby's mud-coated, distressed and hungry brigade bivouacked on ground reportedly twelve inches above water, about two miles from Clarendon, where the gunboat was anchored in midstream. Advised by Colonel Elliot of the vessel's position and armament, an order went out to post a guard around the encampment while urging the men to remain quiet. Most everyone were under the impression they were hiding from imminent danger. For added security, a picket was placed around the town on every road and footpath to detain anyone entering or leaving. At 10 PM, Captain Collins was ordered to see that ammunition chests were filled with solid shot and shells, and to be ready for battle in one hour. Sergeant Francis Coleman Smith from near Lexington was stunned at the order. Other battery members were shocked in disbelief, and strong apprehension of their mission prevailed. Writing after the war he declared, "All had been ignorant of the gunboat's presence except the scouts and a few officers."[26]

At midnight, with Shelby in direct charge, the battery moved out silently and slowly with 400 dismounted rifleman selected from three regiments. Impressed with the danger of the mission, the small column took on the appearance of a somber funeral procession. About a mile from Clarendon, the road emerged from a strip of timber and into an open field. For the first time, the men got a partial view of their objective with

25. Ibid. Frame 0775; Edwards, 266; Testimony given by Acting Ensign J. I. Roberts, August 30, 1864, Frame 0825.
26. Edwards, *Shelby and His Men*, 266; Francis Coleman Smith, "Capture of Gunboat Queen City," *Confederate Veteran* 22 (1914): 120–121.

smoke lazily flowing from twin smokestacks. Shelby quietly ordered the combat team to halt, while the limber chests were carefully uncoupled from the guns. Men were detailed to hand-carry five rounds and powder charges per cannon. The gun carriage wheel hubs were muffled with clothing to insure complete noise discipline in agreement that silence and darkness was all that could save them in the final phase of the unnerving advance. Slowly and cautiously they moved the guns through the darkness down the muddy road while the sleeping monster appeared larger and more forbidding in the closing distance.[27]

At last the outline of buildings became more visible as the gun crews continued dragging their burdens down a street toward the river. Only a brief pause was allowed to study the iron monster serenely veiled in a ribbon of fog, not more than a hundred yards away. A hushed whisper went out for a detail to gather weeds to lay on a bridge that spanned a ditch nearly parallel with the river. Every precaution had to be taken to avoid detection through silence. The task proceeded smoothly until a large fierce dog was discovered who disputed ownership of his portion of ground where the dense growth flourished. He couldn't be induced to move an inch, so he was discreetly allowed his pre-emption rights while the nervous soldiers looked elsewhere.

By 2 AM the 10-pounder rifles were positioned between some dwellings and fifty yards abreast of the *Queen City*. The two Napoleon 12-pounders were placed a hundred yards in front. The immediate area was abundant with dog fennel, four feet high, which lent concealment to the sharpshooters, whose job was to fire into the illuminated portholes. In reference to this scenario Sergeant Smith concluded:

> All our guns were loaded and ready to fire, but we ordered to keep quiet and wait…There we waited for two hours. Think of it! Two hours there with that great monster liable to wake up and annihilate us in a minute! And to give you an idea of how quiet we were, the gun I was with was 20 feet from the

---

27. Smith, "Capture of the Gunboat *Queen City*," 120–121.

front door of a dwelling, and none in the house or boat knew we were within a hundred miles of the place.[28]

Acting Master's Mate William P. Eakle took over the watch from 12 to 4 AM About 3:30, he was alarmed by the neighing of a horse near the edge of the water. Taking a rifle, he stood to the starboard side and tensely waited 15 minutes. Suddenly the roar of artillery exploded into the night from on shore, simultaneously with four distinct flashes penetrating the darkness. This signaled the riflemen, who made short work of the watch that rushed over to the rail to investigate. Eakle at once made his way to the lower deck, to slip the chain. At his gun division he found the lockstrings shorn from the guns, and couldn't find them in the darkness. Collins' shots had extinguished the lamps. Most of the rudely awakened division officers and men were springing to their gun stations, and in a state of undress. Darkness and exploding shells made chaos predominate. After five minutes in the pilot house, Captain Hickey reached the gun deck and personally fired a 32-pounder, then shouted to reload with canister and grape. Regaining the pilot house, some steel plating fell from the ceiling, striking his shins and toes. By now the *Queen City* had discharged four shots from the starboard side.[29]

The engineers were having a full measure of chaos, too, beginning with a projectile breaking the lifter on the starboard engine, disabling it before achieving full operation. The bell then rang to back the port engine, followed by signals to stop, go ahead, and go slow. Splinters and shell fragments were playing havoc with the wires, so Hickey gave orders through a speaking trumpet. While backing with one wheel, the vessel swung to the left and headed downstream with the current. For a few moments Hickey thought he would escape the onslaught, until the unrelenting shore battery placed a projectile into the port engine when

---

28. Ibid., 121; Edwards, *Shelby and His Men*, 267.
29. One end of a lockstring or lanyard was fastened to a heavy circular hammer device mounted on the breach of a naval cannon. When pulled, the string rotated the hammer enough to strike an explosive wafer in the vent tube thus igniting the charge; Testimony given by Hickey, August 8, 1864, Frame 0779.

the tinclad drifted fifty yards. The well-directed shot disabled that engine causing the boat to nose into the willows on the west shore, with the stern quartering upriver. The two 24-pounders in the stern section were never discharged.

On the gun deck, the men stayed at the guns as long as their officers. Deducting those absent from wounds and cowardice, this left few indeed. The Executive Officer, Acting Ensign Fred M. Hathaway, was hardly present at any time and gave no assistance to Captain Hickey. Probably the only officers who remained at their stations throughout were William Eakle, and another brave officer, who suffered three gunshot wounds. With the loyal support of four gunners and the paymaster, Eakle fired three shots portside working the gun as fast as possible in the grim darkness.[30]

Seeing the futility of further resistance, Hickey loudly announced he was going to surrender, and shouted for as many who could do so, to swim ashore and save themselves or be taken prisoner. Giving four blasts of the whistle, he called across the water to his adversary that he had surrendered, and hurried below with the intention of either burning or scuttling the crippled vessel. Upon observing the many wounded, he instead destroyed the signal and general order book. The shaky Hathaway was assigned the dubious task of taking a boat across to make a formal surrender, but he refused. The unpleasant duty was given to none other than the brave Eakle. As four crewman rowed the boat out ten yards, they hesitated and couldn't be induced to go farther, because they feared being taken prisoner. This was frightening to Eakle, because he expected getting shot for their temerity.

Hickey finally took it upon himself to take the boat over with a towline, which was later fastened to a tree. Undoubtedly he experienced much exasperation with each tug of the oars at the situation woven by the unpleasant string of events. He would later learn his craft had taken fifty-four artillery hits during the twenty-minute action, with two missiles

---

30. Testimony given by Acting Paymaster C. S. Sims, Frames 0809–0811 and Acting Masters Mate William P, Eakle, August 30, 1864, Frame 0838.

passing completely through the boat after penetrating both wheel housings. The pilot house, situated topside behind the twin stacks, was completely demolished. Two men were killed and nine wounded. Of the sixty crewman, about twenty-four succeeded in escaping. Captain Hickey was counted with the twenty-five prisoners taken.

Among the prisoners were a number of black crewmen, who were likely recruited from the lower Mississippi. The peacetime Navy had kept their numbers down to one-twentieth of all enlisted men. But by the end of hostilities, 39,000 black sailors were in the service of the U. S and not all were performing menial duties. It's not known how many served aboard the *Queen City*, nine were known for certain to have escaped.

In the next century a former Aide-De-Camp related that some blacks rather than surrender jumped overboard as the boat rounded to, and those who were not killed swam to the opposite shore.

Shelby quickly sent aboard his surgeon and medical attendants, because the enemy medical staff were badly wounded and almost disabled. He then directed removal of the captured property, which included a large payroll. In addition to nine heavy guns, fifty stands of small arms were taken, as well as clothing and commissary stores.[31]

Perhaps the Confederates were elated with the reward of their disciplined efforts in the form of a dreaded gunboat now in their possession in a crippled condition. As it drifted toward their reach in the cool dawn morning, its appearance was certainly in contrast to an hour ago. This feeling of elation gave way to a decline of discipline, combined with deprivation and desire for real food instead of the standard cornmeal and pig grease. Navy rations consisted of dried beans, hard or soft bread

31. Hickey, August 8, 1864, Frame 0786. U. S. Navy Department. *Records of Union and Confederate Navies in the War of the Rebellion*, 31 Vols. (Washington DC: Government Printing Office, 1894–1922), Series I, Vol. 26: 19. Hereafter cited as *ORN*. Unless otherwise indicated, all references are cited from Series I, Vol 26. A stand of arms commonly meant a rifle and cartridge belt. Formally, it meant a complete set of equipment for a soldier, ideally a rifle, belt, a bayonet and an ammunition box. Mark Mayo Boatner III, *The Civil War Dictionary* (New York: David McKay Company, Inc., 1959), 791. *Reminiscences of S. H. Ford, Captain of Company F, 2nd Regiment, Gen. Jos. O. Shelby's Cavalry,1861–1865.* (Typescript in the Missouri Historical Society)

and salted pork. The abundance of good rations went only so far, and undoubtedly Mrs. Sebastian's molasses went down the pipes as well. Clean untorn apparel was well appreciated too—color or branch of service mattered nothing. Attention moved from the wreck and supplies to the prisoners, who were robbed of money and personal effects.

The success of capturing the *Queen City* must be attributed to rigid combat discipline, both by Captain Collins and the 400 dismounted sharpshooters. To the latter especially should go the credit of not prematurely discharging a weapon while awaiting the order to attack. No less can be attributed to Colonel Elliot's recon team ringing the town. From a literal standpoint, scouts on both sides were often the most unreported individuals, whose services frequently spelled the difference between failure and success. Certainly nothing can be taken away from them in reference to events leading up to the capture of the gunboat. The unfortunate Hickey should have kept some pickets of his own across the approaches to the river. In retrospect it should be noted, up to this time, Union vessels were almost never surprised and captured by ground forces. It must be pointed out however, that Hickey on his own initiative did send a reconnaissance through the town, but there was one discrepancy for which he was faulted by the Court of Inquiry—failing to replace his absent Executive Officer with the Senior Officer of Divisions. The Court determined this would have resulted in a more effective firing, but the Court should have also considered the tinclad was simply too vulnerable at close range. That both engines were disabled early attests to this fact.

Chapter Four

A few minutes after the vessel surrendered, a flotilla of nine transports, escorted by three gunboats commanded by 23 year-old Lieutenant George Mifflin Bache, cast loose from DeValls Bluff, thirty miles north of the disaster. General Steele felt threatened by Confederate troop movements toward Pine Bluff and Little Rock, and he literally took to heart General Grant's instructions to protect the line of the Arkansas. Bache occupied the timberclad gunboat *Tyler*, the most formidable gunboat on the White, while accompanied by the tinclads *Naumkeag* and *Fawn*, who were now escorting reinforcements to Steele's right flank up the Arkansas River. The white oak armored *Tyler* was the obnoxious floating fort that gave General Price's division so much grief at Helena.

Lt. George M. Bache. *Courtesy of the U.S. Naval History and Heritage Command.*

Being appraised of the Navy's movements, Shelby redeployed the long arm for renewed flexing which now included a naval 12-pounder and a fine 24-pounder boat howitzer laboriously removed from the *Queen City*. Doubting he had time to off load more, he directed a staff officer to detonate the magazine by firing the boat before sending it adrift. A reverberating explosion signaled her final anchorage a half-mile down river beneath two fathoms of water.[32]

---

32. Fletcher Pratt, *Civil War On Western Waters* (New York: Holt and Company, 1956),

Bache got within ten miles of Clarendon when he was hailed by some escaped sailors who informed him of what happened to the *Queen City*. He turned back the transports and moved ahead, thinking the captured boat might be used in cooperation with the Confederate field battery. When he steamed a few miles farther, he heard two successive reports and noticed a large cloud of black smoke ascending above the trees. Some minutes later, he rounded a bend and sighted the enemy position just five hundred yards distant.

Confederate gunners had been listening with anticipation to the chuffing, bell ringing, and steam whistles, and when the *Tyler* came into view the shore batteries erupted, immediately sending one shot through her pilot house. Almost undaunted, she fearlessly steamed forward, replying with her bow guns until the broadsides came to bear, followed by the *Naumkeag* repeating the same performance. In the intervals between the rounds, the crackle of firearms filled the air as the dismounted brigade aimed for portholes and pilot houses.[33]

The *Fawn* was another matter. Like the *Tyler*, but less fortunate, one of the first missiles also entered the pilot house, but mortally wounding the pilot and carried away the bell wires. In doing so, the engineers erroneously stopped the boat directly under the nearest field pieces, while enduring heavy punishment. A second shot again struck the pilot house, this time tearing up the flooring while throwing splinters in every direction. Another projectile struck between the chimneys, tearing the deck

---

211–13; The number and size of artillery pieces removed from the *Queen City* isn't consistent among Federal sources, thereby reflecting a glow of mystery. Westfall, who was in proximity enough to observe the depletion states: "The Rebels…removed all the arms, most of the ammunition, a 12-pounder howitzer, and the paymaster's stores, and then set fire to the boat. They intended to take the 24-pounder and one 32-pounder to make a battery on shore, but fearing other gunboats would come before they could accomplish it, the project was abandoned." (*ORN*, 418–19). Bache made the incredible assertion: "The enemy had six guns of their own, 10-pounder rifles, 12-pounder smoothbores, and, I think one 6-pounder. Besides these, they used on us a 12-pounder Dahlgren howitzer mounted on a field carriage which they had taken from *Queen* City." (*ORN*, 423). One Missourian noted "We took two of her guns off and planted them on the bank with our own," *Reminiscences of S. H. Ford*.
33. *ORN*, 423.

before smashing a cask filled with water. Finally, three shots entered the casemate on the port side, disabling the crews of two guns. But to the credit of John Grace, Acting Master commanding, it should be stated his crew fired over 100 rounds while enduring the action.[34]

The fleet, by Bache's order, used .25 and .50 second shrapnel projectiles and canister. After the first two gunboats passed a half mile downstream, they rounded to while firing salvo after salvo. The situation on shore became one of desperation as the brigade was being flailed with a brutal crossfire. Nevertheless, the indomitable Shelby and his unyielding regimental commanders were up and down the line shouting encouragement and cheering the dismounted troops. Bache boasted in his after-action report:

> Our fire was terrific; the trees for the space of a mile are marked by our projectiles and low down. When an enemy abandons a light gun he has just captured, and which two men can haul away, he must have been badly used. The whole affair lasted 45 minutes. This vessel was hulled 11 times, doing no damage beyond wounding six men and carrying away a worthless "coffee mill" gun. The boiler casemate stopped a 12-pounder ball. The iron about the *Fawn's* boiler also stopped a shot. The enemy's ammunition was defective, but few of their shots exploding. Besides the howitzer, the following articles were recaptured, viz: Five boxes, 12-pounder shrapnel, 2 boxes 12-pounder shell, 2 boxes 24-pounder shell, 3 boxes 24-pounder shrapnel , 1 box 24-pounder canister, 5 12-pounder shell (fuzed), 2 32-pounder sponges and 1 rammer, 1 24-pounder sponge and rammer. 3 boarding spikes, 2 boats, and 1 anchor with about 30 fathoms of chain.[35]

---

34. Ibid. Acting Masters Mate John Rodgers to Lt. Bache, June 27, 1864, 425.
35. Bache to Phelps, *ORN*, 423; Francis A. Lord, *Civil War Collector's Encyclopedia* (Harrisburg, PA: Stackpole Company, 1963). The Ager gun (or Agar), derisively called the "coffee mill gun," was a single-barrel machine gun that was crank-operated and hopper-fed, resembling a kitchen coffee grinder. The caliber was .58, and designed not to exceed 120 rounds per minute. The Army rejected the weapon, but it received moderate acceptance from Navy officials.

U.S.S. *Fawn. Courtesy of the U.S. Naval History and Heritage Command.*

While the crossfire onslaught was in progress, the Confederate fire diminished. Shelby, unable to inflict more damage in the distressingly unequal contest, ordered a retreat after transferring some of the wounded to nearby homes. Two miles away in their original encampment, the Confederates could evaluate their previous encounter. Shelby's loss in manpower and equipment was not reported, although it may be speculated as having been more severe than the Navy's. Among the wounded was the intrepid Colonel Shanks, who was erroneously reported as having a leg amputated. Casualties among the fleet totaled nine killed and twenty-seven wounded. All the gunboats took some damage. The *Fawn*, temporarily disabled, had to be towed to DeValls Bluff. For the Missouri Brigade, the combat was devastating with one officer writing "… it was one of those fights men shudder over afterward and wonder why any got away."[36]

The first few minutes wasn't difficult for Shelby's Missourians as the gunboats, 200 yards apart, plowed into range past the bend of the narrow river. While the Navy brought into play two bow guns in piecemeal fashion, the gunners in Captain Collins' artillery emplacements enjoyed fire superiority, with their six pieces. This may have been sustained

---

36. Edwards, *Shelby and His Men*, 268.

Captain Richard A. Collins. *Courtesy of the Missouri State Historical Society.*

some minutes longer with the aid of the sharpshooters firing into port openings. If both parties exchanged a broadside, the effect was uncertain due to difficult elevations.[37] When the *Tyler* and her cohort rounded to after having passed, the shoe was on the other foot. The land batteries were receiving fire superiority from more guns getting the range of the blockade. Coupled with the crossfire completed with the *Fawn* upstream, General Shelby could only take satisfaction with the initial belting he had given her and disengage, thus terminating the ghastly dual between two 23 year olds, where one was outgunned and outnumbered at such close proximity.

Gathering all the wounded, Bache took the *Tyler* to DeValls Bluff with the *Fawn* in tow, and communicated with General Steele. He in turn ordered Brigadier General Eugene A. Carr, a West Point man, to organize an expedition to release Shelby's grip from the river. The latter not easily discouraged by the morning's action, decided to construct rifle pits beside the stream that night. These were leveled to the ground the following morning by the *Fawn* and *Naumkeag*.[38]

While maintaining communication with various subordinates assigned to different points of observation, Shelby indicated his next course of action on the afternoon of June 25. A few captured crewmen, Captain Hickey among them, were sent to DeValls Bluff for a proposed prisoner exchange. The remainder were charged to Colonel Dobbins to

---

37. Three separate witnesses testified at the Court of Inquiry that a sloping twenty-foot bluff bordered the river and was obstructive when bearing their guns, including when the crippled *Queen City* was against the west bank. Frames 0778, 0780, and 0798.
38. *ORN*, 427–428.

effect an exchange with the authorities at Helena. Shelby next informed him that he was leaving with the brigade that night, having accomplished everything that could be done at present. He further instructed Dobbins to annoy enemy transports as much as possible navigating the river. However, when the sighting of two gunboats was reported that evening, the decision to withdraw was abandoned in favor of awaiting developments. At 9 o'clock the next day, the *Tyler*, escorting six troop transports, arrived at Clarendon. If Captain Bache put in a belated appearance, he had good reason.

U.S.S. *Tyler*. Painted by F. Muller. *Courtesy of the U.S. Naval History and Heritage Command.*

Chapter Five

General Carr's force and naval escort departed DeValls Bluff the previous day (June 25). Bache was standing in the roundhouse of the *Tyler* when she picked up a log, which carried away the outer wheel housing and quarter gallery. To his indignation, he immediately found himself floundering in the water, unable to swim. He received succor by grasping a piece of driftwood until hauled back aboard his command vessel. He then canceled the expedition until repairs could be completed at the Bluff.[39]

On observing the arrival of the convoy, Shelby's Navy-tested Missourians deployed on each side of the

Brigadier-General Joseph O. Shelby, four months following the Queen City episode. *Courtesy of Wilson's Creek National Battlefield Museum.*

Old Military Road a mile northeast from Clarendon, with the artillery taking position directly on the road. While unopposed, Carr disembarked the cavalry, commanded by Colonel Washington Franklin Geiger, consisting of detachments from the Ninth Iowa, Third Michigan, Eighth Missouri, and the Eleventh Missouri. A squad of twenty-six men of the First Nebraska Cavalry completed the mounted arm. Colonel William H. Graves led forth the infantry consisting of the Eighteenth, Fifty-fourth, Sixty-first, One Hundred-sixth and One Hundred Twenty-sixth Illinois Regiments, followed by the Twelfth Michigan Infantry. Somewhere in

---

39. Ibid.

the column rumbled "D" Battery of the Second Missouri Light Artillery, commanded by Captain Charles Schaerff. With the exception of the Sixty-first Illinois and Twelfth Michigan, none of the infantry had experienced any hard field service. In fact, General Carr later claimed the infantry were unused to skirmishing. Their regimental histories indicated guarding bridges and supply lines with garrison duty in between, and they came onto the field with enthusiasm, for they were about to participate in the kind of action which they had so long been deprived. The majority of the cavalry had been active during the past months, scouting and fighting guerillas. During the past month, they engaged scattered squads of Shelby's horsemen, but now they were to contest each other on a more conventional level. Of Carr's force totaling about 3,000, only 750 represented the cavalry, which formed the spearhead of the expedition.[40]

Eventually Geiger discovered his opponent's skirmish line at the edge of a strip of timber northeast of the town, intersecting the Old Military Road (now State Highway 302). Around 9:30 as the morning waxed hot, there commenced a spirited firefight of thirty minutes' duration. Afterward, Shelby's skirmishers disengaged and withdrew across a 400-yard clearing to the edge of another wooded area adjoining the parent unit.

Having settled into the new position, Captain Collins commenced firing while the opposing infantry came up to support Geiger's cavalry, who may have noticed the oddity of a few enemy horseman wearing sailor's

Washington F. Geiger, 8th MO Cavalry (US). *Courtesy of Green County Archives, Green County, Missouri.*

---

40. Frederick Dyer, *A Compendium of the War of the Rebellion*, 3 vols. (Chicago: Thomas Yoseloff, 1959), 3:684; Mark Christ "Sunstroke & Tired Out: Chasing J. O. Shelby, June 1864," *Arkansas Historical Quarterly* 88 (Summer 2009): 205.

garb, drawing down at them. Almost immediately the crackle of small arms firing became general along the line. Battery "D" was brought into action by the Federals, then Geiger's cavalry wheeled to the right in a flanking movement. Shelby perceived this as an attempt to take his battery and with collars flapping, the Confederates retreated by the cover of the woods to another open field at Pikeville, where the Cotton Plant and Helena road forked. General Shelby probably thought it prudent to move from this exposed position and advanced his brigade five hundred yards further ahead, and placed

Captain James Garrison, Company G, 8th Missouri Cavalry (US). *Courtesy of Wilson's Creek National Battlefield Museum.*

his battery on the road to Cotton Plant, just where it formed the entrance to a large timber slash.

So far, fighting had been taking place on an area of limited size and by opposing forces who were comparatively small. But there was another factor permeating the operation, and that was the oppressive weather. Lieutenant-Colonel John W. Stephens of the Eleventh Missouri Cavalry (US) succumbed to sunstroke just as the skirmishing started. Well would he and others remember that hot June day near Clarendon Arkansas. No record is available concerning how it affected Shelby's force, but the fact these hard bitten veterans were conditioned to operating in all kinds of harsh weather suggests the effect was minimal. Even so, fighting with the sun in their eyes was unpleasant.

After redeploying his troops into a new formation, Carr took a break to pen a report to his fellow New Yorker, General Steele, and to give them a rest. He complained about the infantry being unused to skirmishing and the miserable heat being oppressive. Though he committed a sizable number of troops to pursue his opponent, Shelby's trademark delaying tactics prevented him from bringing all the infantry to bear. As a result some remained in the rear, never firing a shot. The discouraged Carr also suggested a force be sent down from Augusta to rally forth and cut off his wily opponent.[41]

General Carr had positioned his mounted arm on the flanks of his infantry line and slanted forward. Two guns were placed on the far right while two sections of four guns were positioned on Geiger's left, and Carr was now prepared to execute another rear guard assault. Shelby's artillery opened a rapid fire from the woods.

Sgt. Leander Stillwell, 61st Illinois Infantry. *Courtesy of University of Arkansas Little Rock Center for Arkansas History and Culture.*

At one point Private George Lewis of the Twelfth Michigan Infantry, observed:

> We were then Moved forward into a field some 88 or 100 rods through watter from 6 to 24 inches deap. We then halted in the field & the enemy opened on us with their Artillery With good range at about 3/4 of a mile. Their first was wild the second came near our colors & the thirs knocked three of Co. F over. But did Not hurt them for the time.[42]

Union Captain Schaerrf failed to agree, but instead echoed Lieutenant Bache's observation that many of the enemy's projectiles failed to explode. Reporting on his own performance he wrote:

---

41. *ORA*, 1046; *St Louis Daily Missouri Democrat*, July 2, 1864, 1:2; Leander Stillwell, *The Story of a Common Soldier of Army Life in the Civil War, 1861–1863* (Erie, KS: Press of the Erie Record, 1917), 115–116.
42. Christ, "Sunstroke and Tired Out," 207

> Lieutenant Bodungen and I opened at once a crossfire on
> their battery, and after firing 14 rounds every one effec-
> tive, the enemy removed in a hurry, his battery ran into the
> woods in a wild flight, leaving to us two 24-pounder guns,
> which they captured from the Number 26 (*Queen City*)."[43]

Although Schaerff should have been in authority to know the type
and number of guns belonging to his opponent, most all sources con-
tradict him in this regard. The captain may have embellished his report
to sound impressive or was misled by hearsay. Shelby of course made
no mention of his loss in the post-action report, but stated he resumed
his retreat, finding the enemy too strong for him. It was a pitiful day for
horseflesh and a captured 2,500 pound artillery piece.

Throughout the blistering afternoon, Shelby's antagonist continued
to follow him with sporadic rear guard clashes. One detachment more
audacious then the rest were Companies B and G of the Ninth Iowa,
commanded by Major Edgar Ensign. They claimed nearly reaching and
capturing the Confederate general, while giving his personal attention to
the movements of the rearguard. On the opposing side, Monroe County's own Captain William M. Mayo was reported as doing conspicuous
service. With two companies, he soundly repulsed a portion of the Eleventh Missouri (US) on one occasion.[44]

At dark the Missouri general made camp eleven miles from Clarendon
and then moved on, because his scouts brought word that a body of enemy cavalry had landed ten miles below Clarendon and were marching up

43. Ibid; *ORN*, 480; Casto, *Arkansas Late in the Civil War*, 120–121.

44. *ORA*, Vol. 53:479. By far Schaerff's report is the most meticulous account with
regard to movement during the initial pursuit. It is indeed strange that he indicated
the presence of a 6-pounder cannon and two 24-pounder guns. Each Federal account
concerning guns captured only envelopes the subject in a tighter shroud of mystery.
Confederate sources are that of Ford and Edwards. (The latter wrote Shelby's reports).
On his third day out, Carr reported capturing two guns, one navy. The *Memphis Bulletin* of July 2, confirms his claim, reporting that Gen. Carr captured a piece identified
as taken by the enemy during the Camden Expedition. *Memphis Bulletin*, July 2, 1864;
Roster and Record of Iowa Soldiers in the War of the Rebellion, 6 vols. (Des Moines, IA:
Emory H. English, State Printer, 1910), 4:1647; *Biographical and Historical Memoirs of
Eastern Arkansas*, 544.

a road to intercept his retreat. Having remedied this troublesome detail, all remained quiet till midmorning the next day. The Confederates were attacked vigorously and the northeast movement continued up the Old Military Road. Infrequent clashes followed. Five or six miles away on the Munn farm (north side of Brinkley), General Shelby decided he had enough harassment. Quickly massing two regiments, he launched an all-out charge that seemed to scotch the Federals. At any rate they were discouraged from pressing him long enough to cross Bayou DeView, four miles farther up. Carr reported on June 29 that the infantry hadn't touched him since the first day, while also claiming many had their shoes soaked to pieces. The cavalry halted their feeble pursuit at a point eight miles above the Bayou DeView Bridge, or thirty miles from Clarendon. The Southerners had crossed the stream the previous day.[45]

General Carr terminated the pursuit because he found it impossible to catch his opponent, and feared being drawn too far north. In this regard, he thought the enemy should be attacked from Missouri. The infantry commenced the back step on the morning of June 28, and reached the river town during the afternoon the following day. The cavalry kept arriving the following night and noticed the town had been victimized with conflagration. No official reason was given for this misconduct—by 1864 the Civil War had become sordid throughout the South. An Illinois soldier justified the arson as a military measure, because some vacant houses afforded easy cover from which to harass river navigation. Here,

Brigadier-General Eugene A. Carr. *Courtesy of Library of Congress.*

---

45. *ORA*, 1052–1053.

as so often the case, the helpless and displaced civilians were forced to endure the ravages of war.[46]

For Shelby's part, he immediately bivouacked his exhausted command at DeGray's farm in present-day Woodruff County. Here he briefly rested his men and emaciated horses, and placed an order requesting 250 mounts. In a few days, he dispersed his veterans in the field to expedite surveillance and forage needs.

---

46. Stillwell, *The Story of Common Army Life in the Civil War*, 115–116.

Private John R. Sparks, 11th MO Cavalry (US). *Courtesy of Wilson's Creek National Battlefield Museum.*

Chapter Six

Within a month of establishing himself behind General Steele's lines, this Missouri general made his presence painfully known to the Federal Army and Navy. Lt.-Commander Phelps termed him a "daring and enterprising fellow." Privately General Steele had to have expressed much regarding his new found nemesis. Steele made no official description of him. The disastrous Red River Campaign of less than two months previous was unsettling enough. Shelby must have taken the cake by capturing and destroying an enemy gunboat with no losses to himself, but with enemy phases of rescue and pursuit, the odds became greater, and his losses heavier. His total causalities from the beginning until his arrival in Woodruff County likely ranged from sixty to eighty of a speculative force of eight hundred to one thousand men. Carr probably suffered less than half that number while a St. Louis paper reported his loss at five killed and twenty wounded with an unknown figure captured.

In appraising Shelby's retreat from Clarendon, it is noteworthy that the withdrawal was executed with less skill than his advance of a few days previous. In opposition to this, the general was plagued by the following limitations: His horses were reduced before he began the White River enterprise and he was outnumbered three to one. He had twice the number of cavalry on the field as his opponent, but when time came for both sides to deploy for action, the infantry could always come up to replace the Federal cavalry, who in turn could use their mobility to stab his flank. If a Confederate onslaught threatened to endanger the latter, they could always fall back on the infantry for a solid base of support. But most importantly, the primary purpose of Shelby's operation was successfully carried through. His instructions regarding the disruption of White River traffic were for the time fulfilled, leaving General Steele with a deeper realization of the vulnerability of his supply line and that enemy movements toward Pine Bluff and Little Rock were only feints.[47]

An appraisal of Carr's role in the action is difficult. On observation it seems the composition of his force was too prohibitive to destroy his rival, simply because the bulk of it was infantry, and second rate at that. Despite their limitations, they effectively provided timely support when needed.

The impact of the cavalry/navy episode was far reaching, and in early July, the U. S. Navy sent to Clarendon the ironclad *Carondelet*, which mounted thirteen monster guns, including two 100-pounder rifles and three 9-inch guns. This behemoth of 500 tons displacement was especially meant for Shelby if he returned to yank General Steele's supply line again.

In panic, Brigadier General N. B. Buford, commanding at Helena, frantically wired President Lincoln's Secretary of War Edward McMasters Stanton on June 29, making the preposterous assertion that Shelby had cut Steele's land and water communications. General Steele's railroad was never hindered, but strangely, no boats passed Clarendon until June 30. General Carr drove the Missourians from the river community on the morning of June 26, and no blockade had been in force since then. While in command of a paltry force of three hundred cavalry and fewer able bodied infantry, Buford's position on the Mississippi River was highly vulnerable if the Confederates had wanted it. It simply had no strategic value but to protect freed slaves who maintained cotton production and New England tutors. The appearance of captured sailors with the flag-of-truce party was likely the ignition point of Buford's panic. Finally, Helena was far removed from DeValls Bluff and Little Rock.[48] The time-consuming river routes were the only connecting communication lines the Federal authorities shared. Arkansas River navigation was not reliable during the summer months, and Buford thought the White was now closed to him.

---

47. *ORA*, 1042–43.
48. Ibid., 1044–1045.

The ultimate significance of the White River enterprise may lie in the fact that General Shelby's brigade and artillery alone fought a U. S. Navy fleet on a head-to-head basis. An event of such prominence never occurred elsewhere in the War west of the Mississippi River; land forces and a field battery alone making a sustained resistance to "floating forts" armed with devastating six-inch and larger caliber guns. Like other successful cavalry greats of the period, Shelby's military career was a long series of unlikely but well-documented events.

But spectacularity and notoriety are misplaced when not resulting from achieving strategic objectives that would seriously affect the outcome of the war. And like so many other eligible military men, he never got his chance to achieve that level. The final operation of the War for him was to lead the advance of General Price's Missouri invasion beginning on September 19. Price hoped to regain the state for the Confederacy or cause the defeat of Lincoln in the 1864 election, and accomplish a better peace settlement for the South.[49] But Price had no experience leading cavalry, and the botched raid came to a head at Westport (Kansas City). Shelby, the best-suited to lead the invasion, saved the shattered force with fierce rear guard actions far exceeding those conducted anywhere else. Had he the necessary rank to command the 12,000-man expedition, the war might have turned in a different direction.

With the exception of two years spent in Mexico, he lived out the remainder of his life in western Missouri farming for the most part. Shelby died of pneumonia on February 13, 1897 at Adrian, shortly after performing the duties of a United States Marshall for the Western Missouri District, an office he held four years. He was buried in Kansas City. He lived the same number of years after the War as before its outbreak, and was never successful in business, but he possessed extraordinary talent militarily. Thus the short military career was the high point of his life.

Clarendon, however, emerged from the rubble of war as rapidly as other river communities on the White River, and even sent a prominent

---

49. Dean E. Smith, "Price, Sterling," in *Historical Times Illustrated Encyclopedia of the Civil War*, 602.

citizen to the Governor's Mansion (Simon P. Hughes1885-1889). Agriculturally, Monroe County thrived, but cotton remained a staple as in antebellum times. Moving it to market was expedited with a hundred miles of railroad across the countryside. One source claims "Monroe County had better shipping facilities than any other county in the state." The advantage of White River navigation remained steadfast, well into the next century.[50]

Major General Alfred Pleasonton's cavalry deployed as skirmishers, by Alfred Waud. General Pleasonton would later confront Shelby at Westport, Missouri, and in later life made a death bed declaration that Shelby was the best cavalry general in the South. *Courtesy of the Library of Congress.*

---

50. *Biographical and Historical Memoirs of Eastern Arkansas*, 507.

Appendix A

A Partial Roster of Bledsoe's/Collins/6th Missouri Field Battery, Shelby's Cavalry Brigade

R. A. Collins, Captain
Jacob D. Connor, brevet senior First Lieutenant
D. M. Harris, brevet junior First Lieutenant
C. T. Smith, senior Second Lieutenant
J. E. Inglehart, Jr., Second Lieutenant
J. T. Webb, Surgeon
J. S. Williams, Orderly Sergeant
Charles Simmons, First Sergeant
Silas Starks, First Corporal
Charles Tyler, Second Sergeant
Anthony Smith, Second Corporal
Jack Anthony, Third Sergeant
Alec Cooper, Third Corporal
John Cloudsly, Fourth Sergeant
George Pill, Fourth Corporal
John Cooper, Color Bearer, Fifth Corporal
Bugler, Thomas Wilcox, Fifth Sergeant
Peter Hamack, A.Q.M. Sergeant
Artificer, Thomas Alcorn
Blacksmith, Peter Ham
Commissary, Luke Hampton

Privates

James Albinson

George Alexander

Gus, Armstrong

William Bateman

Joseph Beal

Wesly Beal

John Belt

Alfred Bishop

Charles Bishop

Thomas Brittenham

William Camden

John Clark

James Cloudsly

William Coop

Joseph Cooper

Charles Davis

John Dennis

John Doyle

Columbus Elliot

Jeff Elliot

John Fitzgerald

William Grigsby

William Foster

Thomas Graham

Ben Hainline

James Hamilton

Luke Hampton

James Helms

J. Henderson

John Jackson

Alfred Jones

James Lartimer

Jonas Lewis

James Lindsay

Ed McKeever

Evan McManus

Fred Miller

Thomas Minner

John Mooney

John Ninemeyer

Ivan Nolan

James O'Grady

John Paul

Thomas Peltz

William Peters

James Pollock

Thomas Pritchard

William Ray

John Ricketts

Henderson Simpson

Patrick Slade

Thomas Smallwood

William Starks

Eugene Steiger

David Smith

William Smith

William Thomas

Frank Ward

William White

Thomas Windsor

Thomas Wilcox

Peter Youree

Appendix B

Archeological Data

Artifacts from a watery grave.

The survey performed by the Archaeology Division of the University of Missouri-Columbia in 1977, resulted in the following conclusions concerning the wreck site of the U.S.S. *Queen City*:

1. A wooden hulled wreck over 30 meters in length.
2. Preliminary analysis of the recovered artifacts suggest a vessel that was steam driven.
3. No conclusive evidence of any military function for the vessel (i.e., no guns, etc.); a plate of iron encountered on the southern edge of the west hull section suggests the presence of armor plate.
4. The joint use of magnetometric and video instrumental search is mandatory and extremely efficacious in the marginal water conditions.

Appendix C

U.S.S. *Tyler* tied up for repairs on the Mississippi. *Courtesy of U.S. Naval History and Heritage Command.*

Some of the greatest obstacles to river navigation were sandbars and snags, though any hazard could unexpectedly present itself. As previously mentioned the *Tyler's* paddlewheel picked up a floating log which temporarily disabled it on the morning of 25 June, 1864.

During the latter part of April, 1863, the timberclad had to pull out of the attack on Haines Bluff, Mississippi when struck below the water line. This photograph was likely made following the event.

Appendix D

Ten-Pounder Parrott (Army)

Caliber, 3 inches
Length of Tube, 74 inches
Tube Weight, 900 Pounds
Range at 5 degrees Elevation, 1900 Yards

Ten-pounder Parrott Rifle. *Courtesy of the Library of Congress.*

Twenty-Four pounder Dahlgren Boat Howitzer (Navy)

Caliber, 5.82 inches

Shrapnel, 26 pounds

Weight 1300 pounds

Cannister, 14.5 Pounds

Projectile diameter, 5.67 inches

Range at 5 degrees elevation

    Shell (20 pounds): 1270 yards or 0.63 nautical miles

(Ordnance instruction for the US Navy1866).

HOWITZER ON FIELD CARRIAGE

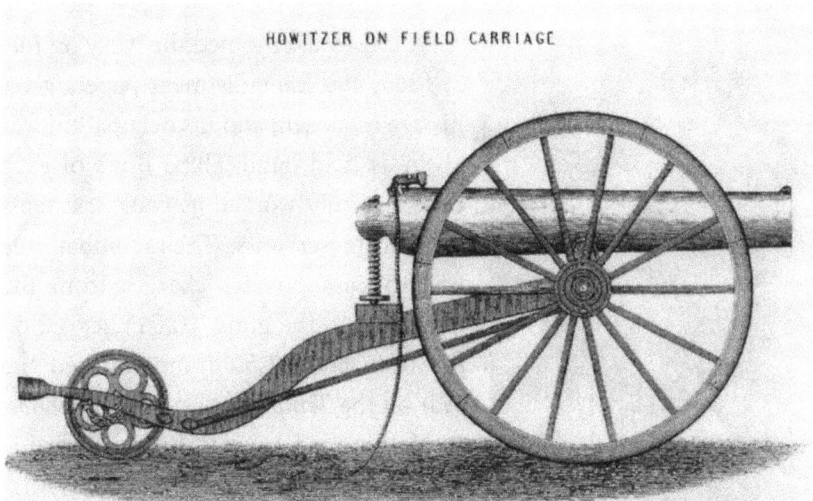

This 24-pounder boat howitzer fired no solid shot and was sometimes referred to as a "shell gun" and was suited to accompany landing parties. Notice the gun lock is in the safety position.

Appendix E

Name and Rank of Black Crewman Rescued by the USS *Tyler*

Robert Booker, Seaman
Fred Buckingham, Landsman
Robert Payne, Ordinary Seaman
Edward Boler, Landsman
Henry Roberts, Landsman

Haden Johnson, Landsman
John W. Smith, Landsman
T. Gazter, Landsman
A. Thompson, Landsman

Robert Walker, 1ˢᵗ Class Boy

Robert Walker (CDV). *Courtesy of Wilson's Creek National Battlefield Museum.*

Young Walker joined the Navy on July 3, 1863, and his enlistment papers gives his age as eleven, and his occupation was given as field hand. Ships Boy's of each class typically worked as cook assistants or officers servants. Their combat role was to pass powder charges from the magazine to the guns. Walker served on the ironclad *Pittsburg* and finished the War on the *Tempest* on August 16, 1865.

Nothing is known of his post war life except he was living in Port Gibson Mississippi in 1895.

A landsman, now an obsolete term, was a sailor with little experience and rated below a seaman and above a Boy First-Class.[51]

51 . William Garrett Piston, Thomas P. Sweeney, M.D., *Portraits of Conflict: A Photographic History of Missouri in the Civil War* (Fayetteville, AR: University of Arkansas Press, 2009), 192.

Bibliography

Government Publications and Records

State:

Office of the Secretary of State, Missouri State Archives. Jefferson City Missouri. *Confederate Home of Missouri, Higginsville, Missouri, Affidavit Applicants*: Junius Terry, Pressly Hall

United States:

General Services Administration. National Archives and Records Service, Military Service Branch, Washington D. C. Compiled Military Service Records—Confederate States Army:
Col. John T. Coffee
Captain Richard A. Collins
Col. W. O. Coleman, 46 Ark Cavalry
Lt. Col. Benjamin Elliot, 9th Missouri Cavalry
Col. Cyrus C. Franklin
Lt. Col. B. Frank Gordon, 5 Mo. Cavalry
Captain Charles Harrison, 10 Missouri Cavalry
Lt. Col. J. C. Hooper, 6 Mo Cavalry
Col. Beal G. Jeans, 12 Mo. Cavalry
Col. David Shanks, 12 Mo. Cavalry
Col. Joseph O. Shelby, 5 Mo. Cavalry
Col Moses W. Smith, 6 Mo. Cavalry

General Services Administration. National Archives and Records Service. *Record Group 109, War Department Collections of Confederate Records*. Records of Shelby's Brigade, Washington D. C.
Letters sent May 19 to September 14, 1864.
U. S. Naval War Records Office. *Official Records of the Union and Con-*

federate Navies in the War of the Rebellion, series I. vol. 26, Naval Forces on the Western Waters, 30 Volumes, Washington D. C., Government Printing Office, 1894–1922.

U. S. War Department. *The War of Rebellion: A Compilation of the Official Records of the Union and Confederate Armies Prepared under the direction of the Secretary of War.* 70 volumes in 128. Washington DC, Government Printing Office, 1880–1901. Series I, Vol. 34.

Records of General Courts Martial and Courts of Inquiry of the Navy Department, 1797–1867, National Archives Microcopy 273.

Newspapers:

Little Rock (Ark.) *Unconditional Union*
Memphis *Commercial Appeal*
St Louis *Missouri Republican*

Periodicals:

Bird, Roy, "Jo Shelby and His Shadow," *America's Civil War* (March 1995): 26–32.

Christ, Mark, "Sunstroke and Tired Out": Chasing J. O. Shelby, June 1864, *Arkansas Historical Quarterly* 88, # 2 (Summer 2009): 201–212.

Ford, S. H., "Recruiting in North Missouri," *Confederate Veteran* 19 (1911): 335.

Marshall, Weed, "Fight to the Finish near Lake, Village Ark.," *Confederate Veteran* 19 (1911): 169.

Hosier, Scott, "'Jo' Shelby Shakes Up Missouri," *America's Civil War* 15 (January 2003): 34.

Monnett, Howard N., "General Jo Shelby and Johnny Ringo," *Westport Historical Quarterly* 7, #3 (December 1971): 25–29.

Redd, O. F. "Service of Gen. Joe Shelby," *Confederate Veteran* 21 (1913): 536.

Smith, Coleman, "Capture of the Gunboat Queen City," *Confederate Veteran* 22 (1914): 120–121.

Books:

Arthur, Anthony. *General Jo Shelby's March.* New York: Random House, 2010.

Breihan, Carl W. *Quantrill and His Guerillas.* Denver: Sage Books, 1959.

Casto, David E. *Arkansas Late in the Civil War: The 8th Missouri Volunteer Cavalry, April, 1864–July, 1865.* Charleston, SC: The History Press, 2013.

Christ, Mark. *Civil War Arkansas: The Battle For a State.* Norman: University of Oklahoma Press, 2010.

Dyer, Frederick A. *A Compendium of the War of Rebellion*, 3 vols. Chicago: Thomas Yoseloff, 1959.

Edwards, John Newman. *Shelby and His Men or the War in the West.* Cincinnati: Miami Printing and Publishing Co, 1867).

Fellman, Michael. *Inside War: The Guerilla Conflict in Missouri during the American Civil War.* New York: Oxford University Press, 1989.

Hale, Donald R. *We Rode With Quantrill: Quantrill and the Guerilla War* Independence, MO: Blue & Gray Bookshoppe, 1998.

Hewitt, Lee Lawrence and Arthur W. Bergeron. *Essays on America's Civil War.* Volume I, Gary D. Joiner, Series Editor. *The Western Theatre in the Civil War.* Knoxville: University of Tennessee Press, 2013.

Johnson, Robert U. and Clarence C. Buel, eds. *Battles and Leaders of the Civil War*, 3 vols. New York: The Century Company, 1887.

Lause, Mark A. *Price's Lost Campaign: The 1864 Invasion of Missouri.* Columbia, MO and London: University of Missouri Press, 2011.

Lee, Fred L., ed. *The Battle of Westport.* Kansas City, MO: Westport Historical Society, 1976.

Mobley, Freeman K. *Making Sense of the Civil War in Batesville, Jacksonport and Northeast Arkansas.* Batesville, AR: P. D. Printing, 2005.

O'Flaherty, Daniel. *General Jo Shelby: Undefeated Rebel.* Chapel Hill: University of North Carolina Press, 1954.

Pratt, Fletcher. *Civil War on Western Waters.* New York: Holt and Company, 1956.

Sellmeyer, Deryl. *Jo Shelby's Iron Brigade.* Gretna, LA: Pelican Publishing Company, 2007.

Smith Jr., Myron J. *Tinclads in the Civil War: Union Light-Draught Gunboat Operations on Western Waters, 1862–1865.* Jefferson, NC: McFarland & Company, Inc., 2010.

Thompson, M. Jeff. *The Civil War Reminiscences of M. Jeff Thompson.* Donal J. Stanton, Goodwin F. Bergquist and Paul C. Bowers, eds. Dayton, OH: Morningside House, Inc., 1988.

www.ingramcontent.com/pod-product-compliance
Lightning Source LLC
Chambersburg PA
CBHW060431050426
42449CB00009B/2244